"Confession time: it is scarier to lead my [...] at my church. As much as I hate to adr [...] is, there are few gospel-centered, acces[...] me lead his kids devotionally. Jessica is a trusted guide to help moms and dads lead their kids to love Jesus."

Darrin Patrick, Pastor, The Journey, St. Louis, Missouri; author, *For the City* and *Church Planter: The Man, the Message, the Mission*

"I am constantly on the lookout for devotionals that are theologically rich, gospel centered, and family friendly. My good friend Jessica Thompson delivers big time. Jessica is concerned to ensure that we (and our children) read the Bible rightly, so we don't end up treating it like a moralistic handbook. Jessica shows that the Bible is one long story of God's meeting our rebellion with his rescue, our sin with his salvation, our guilt with his grace, and our badness with his goodness. In other words, it's fundamentally about Jesus. Thanks to you, Jessica, fewer children will grow up thinking that the focal point of the Christian faith is the life of the Christian."

Tullian Tchividjian, Pastor, Coral Ridge Presbyterian Church, Fort Lauderdale, Florida; author, *One Way Love: Inexhaustible Grace for an Exhausted World*

"I can't think of a better subject to walk through with my family or a better person to walk through it with than Jessica Thompson. *Exploring Grace Together* has a treasure trove of grace reflections and questions at the end of each lesson so that the treasure may be found. Read each devotional, and you will love the Savior in greater ways."

Trillia Newbell, author, *United: Captured by God's Vision for Diversity*

"*Exploring Grace Together* brings the gospel to bear on real-life issues that kids face such as loneliness, jealousy, and failure. Along the way it also calls us as parents to believe that the gospel—not our rules or expectations or kids' good behavior or accomplishments—is truly the power of God for salvation in our kids' lives. That means this book is good news for the whole family."

Nancy Guthrie, Bible teacher; author, Seeing Jesus in the Old Testament Bible study series

"My wife and I have enjoyed journeying through *Exploring Grace Together* with our kids. These forty short, fun devotionals have been kid-tested and proven by the Montgomery boys and girls and by two grateful parents who have often lamented the shortage of books that teach the gospel of God's grace rather than the 'gospel of rules and behavior modification.'"

Daniel Montgomery, Pastor, Sojourn Community Church,
Louisville, Kentucky; co-author, *Faithmapping*

"This book is a special gift to children, parents, and caregivers of children. These brief devotions are packed full of the doctrines and message of the radical, compassionate, and comforting grace of God. They are also deeply practical and applicable to real-life experiences of six- to ten year olds. We wish this book had been available when we were children, but we are very thankful that we will have it for our daughters."

Justin and Lindsey Holcomb, co-authors, *Rid of My Disgrace* and
Save Me from Violence

"Finally—a collection of family devotions centered on the only hope for joy and change that moms, dads, and children have: the gospel of Jesus Christ. In *Exploring Grace Together* Jessica Thompson shares engaging stories, explains key theological concepts, and asks revealing, heart-level questions, all to help your family get beyond therapeutic moralism and powerless application and right to the heart of the Christian faith: the finished work of God's only Son."

Jared C. Wilson, Pastor, Middletown Springs Community Church,
Middletown Springs, Vermont; author, *Gospel Wakefulness* and *The
Pastor's Justification*

"There's nothing I long more to talk with my children about than the life-giving gospel of Jesus Christ. But sometimes I just don't know where to start! *Exploring Grace Together* is a resource for parents *and* kids—creatively and plainly presenting gospel truths. In these devotions Thompson holds up the multifaceted jewel of the gospel and turns it every which way to show off the brilliance of God's grace to us in Jesus Christ. I'm so thankful for this book that leads parents to worship Jesus together with their kids."

Gloria Furman, Pastor's wife, Redeemer Church of Dubai; mother
of four; author, *Glimpses of Grace* and *Treasuring Christ When Your
Hands Are Full*

"Jessica Thompson has written the children's devotional I've been searching for! This is not a book of morality lessons that will leave your kids looking to themselves to do better. Instead, Jessica extends her heart for the freedom of the gospel to your kids as she points them away from themselves and to the lover of their souls. Parents can confidently use this grace-drenched resource with their children, knowing that as they wade through the challenges of the growing-up years they will daily be encouraged in the gospel."

Kimm Crandall, author, *Christ in the Chaos: How the Gospel Changes Motherhood*; mother of four

"In this one-of-a-kind devotional, Jessica faithfully points parents and children alike to the good news that Jesus is bigger than all our mistakes, and his love covers all our sins. Through wise and wonderful storytelling, Jessica helps us discover the free grace available to us in *every* situation because of Jesus's finished work on the cross. Find fresh mercy waiting for your family every day in Jessica's consistent message that we love because he first loved us, and there is absolutely nothing we can do to change God's love for us in Christ Jesus. Give your family the priceless gift of reading this liberating devotional. Our family will be reading it over and over again."

Jeannie Cunnion, MSW; author, *Parenting the Wholehearted Child*

"Kids have problems too. We often try to 'help' our children by minimizing their problems, telling them that things will get better or that they will have bigger issues to deal with when they are older. The truth is that we need to help our children assess and address their hearts from the early years. Their problem may not be that significant, but their heart attitude in response to their problem is of vital importance. Jessica uses simple, real-life issues that adolescents can readily relate to, helps them to see any sinful responses that may exist in their heart, and unfolds gospel truth and the love of Christ in a nurturing way. This is a wonderful book to read as a family to explore together God's amazing grace provided through Christ our Savior!"

Kristie Anyabwile, homemaker; mom; wife of Thabiti Anyabwile, First Baptist Church of Grand Cayman

"Start this devotional tomorrow with your children if you want their hearts comforted, challenged, and compelled to trust Jesus's love to cover all their struggles. Each page leads the whole family to the cross of Jesus—where all of our needs are met."

Trisha R. Wilkerson, author, *Everyday Worship*; biblical counselor; wife of Pastor Mike Wilkerson, Mars Hill, Seattle, Washington; mother of six

Exploring Grace Together

40 DEVOTIONALS FOR THE FAMILY

JESSICA L. THOMPSON

Foreword by
Elyse Fitzpatrick

CROSSWAY

WHEATON, ILLINOIS

Cover design: Connie Gabbert

Cover image: Shutterstock

First printing 2014

Printed in the United States of America

Unless otherwise indicated, Scripture quotations are from the ESV® Bible (*The Holy Bible, English Standard Version®*), copyright © 2001 by Crossway. 2011 Text Edition. Used by permission. All rights reserved.

Trade paperback ISBN: 978-1-4335-3691-5
PDF ISBN: 978-1-4335-3692-2
Mobipocket ISBN: 978-1-4335-3693-9
ePub ISBN: 978-1-4335-3694-6

Library of Congress Cataloging-in-Publication Data
Thompson, Jessica, 1975–
Exploring grace together : 40 devotionals for the family /
Jessica L. Thompson ; foreword by Elyse Fitzpatrick.
    pages cm
ISBN 978-1-4335-3691-5 (tp)
1. Families—Religious life. 2. Christian education—
Home training. I. Title.
BV4526.3.T475   2014
249—dc23   2013033437

Crossway is a publishing ministry of Good News Publishers.

VP		24	23	22	21	20	19	18	17	16	15	14
15	14	13	12	11	10	9	8	7	6	5	4	3	2	1

To Wesley, Hayden, and Allie

My love for you grows more each day.
I thank God for the sheer delight of being your mother.

Contents

Foreword

In 2011 Crossway published *Give Them Grace: Dazzling Your Kids with the Love of Jesus.* That book was a collaboration between my daughter, Jessica Thompson, and me, and in it we sought to take the truths of the gospel that we have both come to love so dearly and apply them to parenting.

You see, both of us had been growing in our understanding of how the work that Jesus has already done should color and motivate how we think about ourselves and how that new identity *in* Christ should transform the way we live. But we weren't sure how it would transform parenting. The truth is that we were learning as we went—she more than I because she homeschools three kids. For her, it's where the rubber meets the road; it is life in the trenches.

So we began to write *Give Them Grace.* There were days when I would write something and send it to her to read and comment on. I didn't have little children around to be my guinea pigs, and although I knew that my thoughts were correct theologically, I wasn't sure how they would work practically. So I would send her a few pages and ask,

"Does this make sense? How would you do this with your kids?" After a while I'd get an answer, and the beauty of how the gospel invaded life around a swimming pool or in the classroom or on the baseball field became plain for me to see. Jessica was learning something I didn't know: she was learning about the intersection of justification and fights over Optimus Prime (in case you don't know, he's the big boss Transformer), and she was learning it well enough to communicate it to her three kids.

Since that time, Jessica and I have had many opportunities to present the truths found in *Give Them Grace* to parents around the country. So many parents have thanked us for freeing them from the terrible burden of what we call the Parenting Covenant of Works—you know, *good parenting in, good kids out*. That paradigm is crushing Christian parents all over the country, and they're so happy to hear that they can enjoy their children again and partner with them as they run to Jesus and fight sin and unbelief together. We're so thankful for the work God is doing through that book.

But one request we've heard over and over again is, *How would you do this in family devotions? How would you tell your children about the gospel? How do we talk about the Bible and still remember the work Jesus has done?*

This book is the answer to those requests, and Jessica is the right person to write it. She knows how the gospel transforms sinners because it has transformed her, and she knows how to communicate those deep truths to children because she's done it for years. I've watched her while I fumble for words and think, *Surely I should have something to say about the gospel here*. I've watched her lean into her children and—in weakness, humility, and faith—break the bread of life with them.

I'd like to say that Jessica learned this art from her dad and me, but that's not the truth. The truth is that she learned about this grace from the Lord of grace, who has gifted her with great love for children and an ability to communicate the gospel in words they can understand. And so it's my hope that thousands of parents around the world will pick up this book and the truth it represents. Like us, children need good news. They need to be freed from the moralistic, therapeutic deism that has colored our parenting for generations. Give your children the gospel— not just once but over and over again—and then trust the Savior to work in their hearts to grant them faith to believe and love to serve.

—Elyse Fitzpatrick

Treasure Hunt

What if I told you we were about to go on a treasure hunt? Would you think, *Wait a minute, I thought we were about to read a book about the Bible*? Well, that is true; you are going to read a book about the Bible. But in this book I am going to take you on an adventure—an adventure that could change the rest of your life, an adventure in which we are going to be looking for the greatest treasure we could ever have. This treasure isn't money, but it is worth more than money. This treasure is Jesus, the only treasure that will ever give you everything you need. We are going to look for Jesus at school, at home, in sports, in music—everywhere. You may think that Jesus and talk about God are only for church, but on our treasure hunt I am going to show you how he can be found in whatever you are doing.

On our treasure hunt I might use words that you don't understand. I also might talk about Jesus in ways that you just don't get. When you come to those places, be sure to ask those with whom you are reading this book to help you. Hopefully they will be able to make it clear for you.

I am going to tell you stories about kids just like you, kids your age, kids that like the same things you do, kids that get angry and sad just like you do. Then we are going to see how our treasure, Jesus, helps them and gives them everything they need.

The most important part of our quest is asking for God's help. I can give you the right map, but only he can make you see where the treasure is. So why not stop right now and ask God to open your eyes to see this treasure that we are talking about?

Okay, are you ready? I hope you are excited, because you are about to see that the most beautiful treasure can be yours if you just believe.

Dear Parents,

I am so excited that you have decided to take part in this treasure hunt with your child. I do have a couple of items I would like to discuss with you. First, this is not a cure-all for your kids' disobedience. Your children are real human beings with real hearts, and they need the work of the Holy Spirit to change them. You won't be able to read these devotions and then expect your children to be different people the next day. That's not how you work, and it is not how your kids respond. How often have you heard a wonderful, convicting sermon and then gone and returned to your sin on Monday? Change is a slow process for children, just like it is for you.

There are questions at the end of each devotional. I know from experience that asking kids spiritually minded questions can end up in anger and frustration. There are times, maybe even the majority of times, when they are unresponsive or not listening or just don't care. During those times, your work is not to convince them of the importance of what you are doing but rather to lean into the Holy Spirit. You won't be able to come up with the right words to make a hard heart soft. That is God's work, so ask him to do it. You don't want to take this devotional and beat your kids over the head with it. If you are depending on it to save your kids, you will end up being angry or full of despair when they don't respond the way you want. So if you are feeling angry or despairing because your children aren't where you want them to be, repent and remember that God is the author of all salvation.

One last thing: don't give up on your kids. You don't know how God may use this book. Your kids may be unresponsive initially, but God may choose to use it later. If they don't seem to want to answer the questions, maybe you could answer them from your own life.

My prayer is that you and your children will see the gloriousness of the gospel of grace, that you will together be equipped to push this gospel into every area of your lives, and that you will see his grace is truly sufficient in your weakness.

Grace and Peace,
Jessica

1

The Bad One

None is righteous, no, not one;
    no one understands;
    no one seeks for God.
All have turned aside; together they have
      become worthless;
    no one does good,
    not even one.

ROMANS 3:11–12

Shane can't understand why he always seems to do the wrong thing. He knows he isn't supposed to lie, but he did anyway. He knows he isn't supposed to cheat, but he just couldn't seem to keep his eyes off Lisa's paper. Sometimes he looks around at his other friends and thinks he is always the one being bad. He especially feels this way at home. His mom and dad love God and always talk about Jesus, and they read their Bibles. His older brother Jim is the good one. He is the one everybody seems to love because he always does the right thing. Shane feels that he is the only bad one. He feels that since he always does the wrong thing, he just isn't going to try to do the right thing anymore.

What Shane doesn't believe is what our passage, Romans 3:11–12, says. He doesn't believe that everyone is bad and that no one understands or looks for God. Maybe you feel the same way Shane does. Maybe you feel that you always do it wrong. The Bible agrees with you on that one, and that may feel like bad news. But that is not all the news the Bible gives. There is also some really good news. It's about our treasure, Jesus. The really good news is that Jesus loves sinners. Jesus loves people who aren't doing the right thing. Does that surprise you? It surprises me! The good news of the Bible is that Jesus came to love and rescue people who don't love him. I know when people don't like me, I want to stay away from them, but Jesus does the opposite of that. Don't let your badness keep you from joining us on our treasure hunt. Don't think you are the only one who does the wrong thing; we all do the wrong thing. Jesus loves you anyway. He will forgive you. He wants to be nice to you; he wants to be your treasure.

EXPLORATION TIME

1) Do you ever feel like Shane? When you do feel like him, what do you do?

2) When you do something wrong, do you want to hide from God and your parents?

3) What should you remember about Jesus when you think you are too bad to go to him?

4) What is the good news or treasure of our story today?

Take some time now to pray that you will understand and believe that Jesus wants to be your friend. Believe that he came to save you from the fact that you can't live right.

2

The Good One

For all have sinned and fall short of the glory
of God.

ROMANS 3:23

For the wages of sin is death, but the free gift
of God is eternal life in Christ Jesus our Lord.

ROMANS 6:23

Rita is the sweetest girl most people have ever met. At least, that is what she hears all the time. She is almost always polite, almost always nice, and almost always obeys her parents. Most adults notice these things, and they are sure to tell Rita and her parents what a great job they are doing. The only problem is that Rita knows something isn't right. Rita feels angry a lot of the time, especially when other people don't follow the rules or when her parents tell her she is doing something wrong. She feels that if she is trying so hard to be good, other people should try to be good too. She also can't understand why her parents always have to point out the few bad things she does, especially since she is so good most of the time.

Rita's problem is that she doesn't really believe Romans 3:23 and 6:23. There are two very important parts to our treasure map in those verses. Do you see them? First, all have sinned. That "all" includes whoever is reading this, whoever is listening; and it includes me. Rita knows that sometimes she does things that aren't exactly right, but she doesn't really think of herself as a sinner who deserves death.

Rita also doesn't believe the second clue to our treasure. There is a free gift waiting for her (and for you) just to snatch. It doesn't cost one single penny; you don't have to do anything to earn it, and you can't do anything to buy it. All you have to do is believe. Rita has been trying to buy this free gift with all the good things she does. She has been thinking that if she is just good enough, then everybody will say nice things about her and God will love her and give her life forever with him. But God doesn't want her or you to try and earn his free gift; he just wants to give it. He loves giving, and he loves being generous.

God has a job, which is to give, and we have a job, which is to receive. Rita has been thinking her treasure is what other people think of her. Jesus wants Rita and you to know that the real treasure is what he thinks of you and how he loves you. He wants to give you himself and life forever with him, but you must believe that is true. You must believe that you sin and that your sin earns death. You also must believe that nothing you can do can earn the free gift. It's free! He loves to give to you. You must believe that he is as good and generous as he says he is.

EXPLORATION TIME

1) Do you ever feel like you have to earn God's love?

2) Do you believe the two parts of our verses?

3) Which part is harder for you to believe?

4) If you have a hard time believing all that's in today's verses, you can pray right now and ask God to help you believe.

3

The Secret

> For I am sure that neither death nor life, nor
> angels nor rulers, nor things present nor things
> to come, nor powers, nor height nor depth,
> nor anything else in all creation, will be able to
> separate us from the love of God in Christ Jesus
> our Lord.
>
> ROMANS 8:38–39

Paige has a secret. The secret is about something she has
done. She has done something very wrong, and her secret
is making her feel awful. She feels that she can't tell people,
because they won't love her anymore. She is really scared
of getting into loads and loads of trouble, too. So Paige
keeps her secret hidden away in her heart. And although
she never speaks of it, it is always there, like a giant mountain that she just can't seem to get away from. Everywhere
she turns, it seems as though the giant mountain is right in
front of her, threatening to hurt her. Paige thinks that nothing she can do will make the mountain go away. Paige is
right—there is nothing she can do, but there is something
God has already done.

Paige needs to hear Romans 8:38–39. Paige especially needs to hear the very end of this passage, ". . . nor anything else in all creation, will be able to separate us from the love of God in Christ Jesus our Lord." What Paige doesn't believe is that even though her secret is big, God's love for her is even bigger. God's love makes the biggest secret mountain seem like a tiny anthill when compared to his love.

He promises that nothing will change his love for you if you are one of his children. There is nothing and no one stronger or bigger than God's love for his family. His love never stops; it never gives up on you. The things you do can't make him love any less. All you have to do is believe he is as loving as he says he is, even though you know you don't deserve his love. He loves you because he sees you *in Jesus Christ*. That means that when he looks at you, he sees only his perfect Son, Jesus.

You see, not only is God our treasure, but we are his treasure too. His love for his treasure is perfect, and it never changes—ever. Kind of hard to believe, right? Our God is just that good and that kind.

EXPLORATION TIME

1) Do you have a big secret mountain that seems so big that nobody can love you?

2) Do you believe that there is something one of God's kids could do that would make God love him less?

3) Do you understand what the Bible means when it says, ". . . in Christ Jesus our Lord"? If not, ask the adult reading with you to explain it.

4

Just Not Sure

For by grace you have been saved through faith. And this is not your own doing; it is the gift of God.

EPHESIANS 2:8

Sam thinks he is different from everybody else. The reason he feels different is that he isn't sure if he believes the way his parents do. When he goes to church, he questions if what he is learning in Sunday school is true. He feels bad that he isn't excited about God like everyone else is. He just can't be sure that the God of the Bible is true; he feels that some of those Bible stories are just too crazy to be true. He doesn't feel that he can talk to anybody about his thoughts and doubts. He feels sure that nothing anybody could say or do could change his mind.

Sam is right about one thing: there is nothing anybody can say or do to change his mind. Ephasians 2:8 tells us why: faith to believe is a gift from God. *Faith* is a bit of a fancy word, isn't it? It might be a little hard to understand. Let me explain it. Faith is when you are sure—absolutely sure—that something is true. When you are about to sit on a chair, you have faith that the chair will hold you. You are sure that when you sit down, you won't go flopping onto the ground. Now, faith in God is a bit like sitting in a chair. Faith in God is when you say you believe the Bible and that everything in it is true. It is believing that the treasure map will get you to the treasure.

Here is what is very special about Ephesians 2:8: there is nothing you can do to make yourself believe in God. That thought should make you giddy, because the hard work isn't up to us. God does the hard work for us. He gives us the faith we need to believe. We know that God loves to give gifts to his kids. He is excited to share himself with you. He proved this because he gave his Son, the thing he loved most, to you. God wants to give you the gift of faith. He wants to give you and Sam everything you need to believe.

So what should Sam do? What should you do? All we have to do is ask for faith. Ask God to give you that special gift that will help you believe he is real. I have faith that if you ask, he will give. He is just that good, and that kind, and that loving.

EXPLORATION TIME

1) Do you ever have questions about what you learn at church? If yes, what are they?

2) Do you sometimes wonder if God is real?

3) Do you want to pray and ask God for the special gift of faith?

5

The Center of Attention

Because your steadfast love is better than life,
my lips will praise you.

PSALM 63:3

Lilly loves to be loved. She is funny and is always having fun. People generally like being around her. If you ever hear people laughing loudly, you know Lilly is with that group, making silly faces or telling funny jokes. Lilly seems always to have a smile to share.

The truth is that she is very sad on the inside. She feels that she has to be funny and nice in order to make people love her. She thinks that her friends are her treasure. Sometimes Lilly gets angry because she thinks her friends don't love her enough. She thinks that maybe they like her other friends more than they like her.

Lilly needs to be reminded of the best love that has ever existed.

There is a love that is better than living. There is a love

for you that is always there. Do you see the word "stead-fast" in our verse, Psalm 63:3? That is another fancy word. Let me explain it. *Steadfast* means there is nothing you can do to change that love. It's like a big tree that has been around forever, and no matter what anybody does to try to move the tree, it just stays there. You can push on it and kick it and do all sorts of things, but the tree just stays right where it is, where it will always be. That is what God's steadfast love is like. God's love is the greatest treasure. It is better than anything you can think of. It is better than having all the friends you want or all the video games you want. It fills you up all the way to the top. Lilly feels like she has to be nice and funny all the time or she will lose the love of her friends. She can't do anything to mess up God's love for her.

The really cool thing about his love is you don't have to work hard to keep it. That should make you want to shout, "YIPPEE!" and do exactly what our verse says next: "My lips will praise you." Knowing about his steadfast love will make our hearts happy and our mouths want to say nice things about him. The truth is our hearts won't be happy with anyone's love but God's. Until we can be happy with God's love, we will always want more and more people to love us. Even when we think that our friends' love is the most important, God's love really is, because it doesn't change. He just loves you that much. He is just that kind, and he is just that good.

EXPLORATION TIME

1) Do you ever feel that having your friends' love is the most important thing?

2) Is it hard to remember that God's love is your real treasure? Why?

3) When you forget that God's love is the best, what can you do to remember?

6

No One Gets Me

For we do not have a high priest who is unable to sympathize with our weaknesses, but one who in every respect has been tempted as we are, yet without sin.

HEBREWS 4:15

Trey is certain that no one understands him. He feels that he is going through everything all by himself. It is true that Trey has had a hard life. His dad and mom are divorced. His dad left their family, and his mom now has to work all the time. He has to stay at school every night until it is dark, waiting for his mom to come and get him and his sister. He hates how tired she always is. He wants to talk to her about school and what happens there, but she always tells him she is too busy to even think. He feels that he has no friends, no one who really knows what his life is like. He knows his mom loves him, but he really wants someone to listen to him. Trey knows about Jesus; his mom takes him to church every Sunday. But just like everyone else, Jesus seems far away, and Trey feels alone.

He thinks there is nobody who really wants to take care of him.

Trey doesn't know how much Jesus loves and cares about everything that happens in his life. Trey does not know what our verse, Hebrews 4:15, says. When our verse talks about a "high priest," it means someone who cares about every detail of your life; someone who talks to God for you, someone who can take care of your sin. Jesus knows exactly how Trey feels. Jesus had to become a boy, so he understands what it is like to have no one who understands you, no one to talk to.

Jesus was so different from everybody else. He had no sin; he never did anything wrong. Have you ever been around people who always seem to be good? It's kind of hard to be with them, isn't it? Well, Jesus was the one who was always good, and people hated that so much that they eventually killed him. Even though Jesus was always good, he had to fight against sin. He had to fight against being sad and angry that no one understood him. Trey wants someone who understands; he doesn't know that Jesus is that person. Jesus understands all the hard things we go through. He really knows how we feel, and he cares for us.

There is a big word in our verse—sympathize. That word means Jesus wants to share all the hard things in your life. Most people only want to share good things, but he wants to share everything. He really feels what you feel and hurts when you hurt, and loves you always.

EXPLORATION TIME

1) Do you ever feel that no one understands you?

2) Do you ever feel that no one cares about what you go through?

3) Do you have any friends like Trey that you can be a friend to?

4) How does knowing that Jesus cares for you help when you are sad?

7

I Can't Be Nice

But God shows his love for us in that while we
were still sinners, Christ died for us.

ROMANS 5:8

Annie is having a really hard time being nice to Priscilla.
Priscilla is always mean; everything she says is unkind. She
is like a thorn that gets stuck in your sock. Even though she
just makes little comments, they sting and irritate Annie.
Annie knows she should be nice; she knows the right thing
to do, but she just doesn't want to do it. She wants to be
mean back; she wants to show Priscilla what it feels like to
be hurt by what someone says. Annie wishes they didn't
have to be around each other, but they go to the same church
and the same school. Annie knows she has never been that
mean to anybody, and she can't understand why Priscilla is
that way. It's like Priscilla wants to be everybody's enemy.
Annie tries to do what her parents say—she tries to pray for
Priscilla—but she just doesn't like her one bit.

Our verse, Romans 5:8, is the only thing that will help
Annie's heart feel soft when she thinks about Priscilla. This

verse tells us what we were like when God chose to love us. It tells us about ourselves when Christ chose to die for us. Here is how it describes you and me: "While we were still sinners . . ." It doesn't say, "When we had decided to be nice," or "When we had decided to love God"; it says, "While we were still sinners." While we were disobeying God, while we were his enemies, he decided to show us love. He decided to give us his treasure, his Son. Can you imagine giving your most important treasure to someone who hates you or to someone who is always mean and does the opposite of what you say, all the time? Well, this is exactly what God did for us.

Now, you might be asking yourself, what does that have to do with Annie and Priscilla? Let me tell you: the only way Annie will ever be able to love Priscilla is if she remembers how much God loves her even when she doesn't deserve it and when she isn't nice. Annie must remember that God still loves her even though she doesn't always obey or do the right thing. God gave her his best treasure, and he will continue to give her everything she needs even when she is ungrateful and complains and wants more. If Annie can remember this, she will be able to love Priscilla without expecting Priscilla to be nice back. If she can remember God's love, then she will be able to show that same love to Priscilla.

EXPLORATION TIME

1) Is there anybody in your life that you have a hard time being nice to?

2) Do you think that remembering God's love for you will help you when people are being mean? Why or why not?

3) Take some time right now and pray that God would make your heart soft toward whoever it is that is a bit difficult. Pray that he would help you to see his amazing love for you so that you can love others.

8

Completely Alone

Greater love has no one than this, that someone lay down his life for his friends.

JOHN 15:13

Marcus is a lonely boy. Every morning he dreads getting up and going to school. He hates it so much that he often pretends that he is sick so he can stay home. He tries to be by himself at school, which is much easier than being around all the other kids. For the most part, the kids in his class ignore him because he seems so quiet and weird. Sometimes, though, a group of kids makes fun of him and call him mean names that hurt his heart so much he thinks he might actually die. He eats lunch by himself and tries to find the corner of the playground to hide in. Being at home isn't much better than being at school. He is an only child, and none of the neighbor kids are nice to him. He sees them playing together outside but is too afraid to go and play with them. Church is a little better because all the parents make the kids be nice, but it is still sad for him.

Marcus is in desperate need of a friend, a friend who will stand next to him and stick up for him. Marcus thinks he will never have a friend who will help him at all.

But Marcus already has this friend. Marcus has a friend who loves him so much that this friend actually died in order to be his friend. This friend cares for Marcus, even though Marcus doesn't really pay much attention to him. Marcus doesn't know that Jesus calls him a friend. Jesus is the one who knows everything about Marcus. He knows every thought, and he knows everything Marcus loves and everything Marcus hates. He knows what Marcus is scared of, and he is the friend who is there for him. Jesus's love for Marcus is the best love in the world.

Jesus cares about every single thing that happens to each of us. Jesus and his Father love us so much that they decided to do the most loving thing that has ever been done in all of history. They decided that Jesus would come and live as a human and experience loneliness and being made fun of. Jesus would do that without sinning against anyone, and then he would die on the cross for every time we make fun of someone or ignore someone. He would live the life we needed to live and pay for our sins. He did this because he is our friend. He is the only friend we will ever need, and the really good news is he is the friend we will have forever.

EXPLORATION TIME

1) Do you ever feel lonely like Marcus did?

2) Are there any kids you can think of who don't have many friends, who seem a little lonely?

3) Thinking about Jesus's love for his friends will help you not to be lonely, and it will help you to be able to love those who are lonely.

4) Have you ever thought of Jesus as a friend?

9

Best Friends

Those who were not my people I will call "my
people," and her who was not beloved I will call
"beloved."

ROMANS 9:25

MaryAnn and Wanda were the best of friends. They did
everything together. They had matching shoes, matching
shirts, matching earrings, and a best-friends necklace. And
then Natalie moved next door to Wanda. That is when the
trouble started for MaryAnn. MaryAnn became sure, absolutely positive, that her best friend—her most important
relationship—was gone. Now Wanda and Natalie play together more and more, so MaryAnn has decided she will
just stay at home. She thinks being by herself is easier than
trying to figure out if Wanda still loves her or if Natalie
even likes her. MaryAnn feels lonely and sad and that she
isn't anyone's special somebody anymore.

MaryAnn had made Wanda her treasure and decided
that being Wanda's BFF was the best thing in the entire
world. So when Wanda got a new friend, MaryAnn thought
her treasure was lost. MaryAnn doesn't know that she is

already someone else's treasure. She has forgotten that God has called her his, and that she is his beloved.

The word *beloved* in our verse, Romans 9:25, is a very special word indeed. It means that God's kids, like me and you, are much-loved. We are his sweetheart; we are his darling. He thinks of us this way because of what Jesus has done for us. Jesus came to earth to live the life we were supposed to live and to die the death we were supposed to die so that God could look at us and say, "My darling, my beloved, and my friend."

MaryAnn knows that God loves her, but that feels so far away when she is with Wanda and Natalie. She feels completely unloved when she is with them. What Mary-Ann needs is to pray that God will remind her that she is actually loved more than she could ever imagine or dream or hope. Then she can love God back. Not only will she love God, but also she will be able to love Wanda and Natalie too. She won't always have to worry if Wanda loves her, because she will be absolutely sure that God does, and his love is the absolute best love ever. She will be able to be friends with Wanda and Natalie without always thinking about herself, because she will know God is thinking about her, his beloved.

EXPLORATION TIME

1) Is it hard to believe that God calls you his beloved?

2) How is it possible for God to call you "beloved" when you don't love him all the time?

3) Are there any friends or relationships that you have made into your treasure?

4) Do you think remembering our verse when you feel left out will help you?

10

A Feeling-Low Kind of Day

Likewise the Spirit helps us in our weakness. For we do not know what to pray for as we ought, but the Spirit himself intercedes for us with groanings too deep for words.

ROMANS 8:26

Samantha sits alone and confused in her room. She has had a terrible day at school and things haven't gotten any better since arriving home. Nothing big happened; it has just been one of those days when you feel that something is wrong, the sort of day in which everything bothers you and you feel angry. Samantha knows the only thing that will help her now is God. Her mom told her that maybe she should pray for help. So here Samantha sits, feeling that she doesn't know what to say or do. Her parents have told her that talking to God is just like talking to a friend, but that isn't helping much. She still doesn't know how or what to pray. Every time she tries to pray, she keeps thinking about food or dogs or toys. She can't keep her mind on praying. This is very frustrating, and Samantha wants to give up.

Our verse, Romans 8:26, is just for Samantha. It contains some words that might be hard to understand, but it is important to understand because the verse has such a brilliant treasure that you will want for the rest of your life.

First, our verse says that we don't know how to pray. Do you ever feel that way? I know I do. I don't know the right words to say; my mind is always going offtrack, just like Samantha's. That doesn't mean we should give up, though. Once again, we have good news. We see in our verse that the Spirit is praying for us, which is what that fancy word "intercede" means. He is really praying for us. He is praying with just the right words. His heart is so full of love for you that he doesn't even use words. There are no words to tell how he feels.

So when you sit down to pray, you don't have to use fancy words or say just the right thing. All you have to do is talk about your heart and your day. Just tell God that your day was a big, rotten mess, and then the Spirit will help you. He prays for you. He loves on you and reminds you that even though you had a bad day, you are still his treasure.

EXPLORATION TIME

1) Does praying feel too hard?

2) Do you believe that the Spirit can help you when you pray?

3) What are some things you want to pray about now?

11

The Brothers

> In this is love, not that we have loved God but
> that he loved us and sent his Son to be the pro-
> pitiation for our sins. Beloved, if God so loved
> us, we also ought to love one another.
>
> I JOHN 4:10–11

Everything—and I mean everything—Jermaine does is
bothering his older brother Keenan. These two brothers
have times when they really get along, times when they
laugh and play. Right now is not one of those times. Right
now is a time of anger and annoyance. Jermaine knows
exactly what to do to make Keenan angry, and he has done
it. Keenan has decided that Jermaine is out to get him in
trouble, so everything Jermaine does, Keenan is taking
the wrong way. Keenan is being extremely touchy, and
the two brothers are fighting nonstop. Their fighting is
making it really tough for the rest of the family to enjoy
any time together. Keenan and Jermaine don't like this,
but they think there are just too many hurt feelings to act
any differently. They both are sick of trying to be nice,

only to have the other one be mean. At least that is what they think.

Keenan and Jermaine need help, and the help they need is found in 1 John 4:10–11 this week. They both need to be reminded about the love God has for his people. You see, God's love started it all. God's love is what makes us love him. God decides to love us, and then we get to love him back. God's love chased us down when we didn't love him. God's love found us when we tried to hide. God's love gave Jesus to be a propitiation for our sins. That's a big, fancy word, isn't it? *Propitiation* means "anger taker awayer." That is what Jesus did for us. He took away all of God's anger toward all of our sin. We didn't deserve his anger to be taken away, but Jesus took the anger of God when he died on the cross. So right this very second, God feels absolutely no anger toward you.

What is very interesting about our verse is that it tells us all about how Jesus came to show us God's love. Then it tells us what the thought of God's love should make us do: God's love should make us want to love others. Now, because our minds and hearts don't always work just right, we still hurt others by not loving them. But what we need to remember is that even when we don't love, God still loves us. His love is always running after us and finding us. His love gives us everything we could ever need. Jermaine and Keenan can love each other because they have been loved by the best; they have been loved by God.

EXPLORATION TIME

1) Do you know that God loved you before you were even born?

2) Are there any people in your life that you have a hard time loving?

3) How can thinking about God's love for you help you to love the unlovable people in your life?

12

The Fighting Family

> Because you are sons, God has sent the Spirit of
> his Son into our hearts, crying, "Abba! Father!"
> So you are no longer a slave, but a son, and if a
> son, then an heir through God.
>
> GALATIANS 4:6–7

Kyle is hiding in his closet again. Most evenings, this feels
like the best place to be. His mom and dad keep yelling at
each other, and he doesn't know what to do. He feels angry
and sad and scared. One thing he doesn't feel is safe. He
can't understand why his parents don't get along. He feels
that if he was just a better boy, if he got better grades or
never disobeyed, maybe his mom and dad would not be
so mad all the time. Kyle tries to remember to pray, but
God feels so far away. Besides, whenever he starts to pray,
all he can hear are their loud voices arguing. Kyle feels that
he doesn't belong, that he doesn't have a family.

Kyle needs our passage, Galatians 4:6–7. He needs to
know that he has a heavenly Father who cares for him.
God has adopted Kyle; God is his Forever Daddy. Now, this
may sound a bit strange to you. It may seem that God is far

away because he is big and powerful. But God wants you to think of him as you would think of the best dad in world. He is close; he loves to hear about your day. He loves to hear about your stories and dreams. God has looked at you and loved you. He has decided that he wants you in his family. You don't have to think of God as a big, powerful master whom you have to always obey—or else! He is not standing up in heaven thinking of you as a slave who has to get his work done. He is in heaven looking down on you lovingly, as a father looks at a child he loves. He calls you his own kid. He gives us rules because he knows what is best for us. He loves to see us happy and safe. Following his rules is always the best.

Kyle needs this Bible passage because his family is a mess. Your family might be having trouble or it might be A-ok. Either way, you need this passage. The most important family you belong to is God's family; it will last forever. God loves you better and stronger than any dad or mom here on earth ever could. He loves you this way because of Jesus Christ. If you believe that Jesus lived perfectly for you and took the punishment you deserve, you have a forever hiding place. You are hidden in Christ. When God looks at you, he sees only what his Son has done. God loves you just as much as he loves Jesus. He has adopted you to be in his family as Jesus's brother or sister. So now Kyle and you and I can all run to our Heavenly Father. He loves us and takes care of us.

EXPLORATION TIME

1) Does God seem more like a master than a dad?

2) Did you know that Jesus is your brother?

3) Does thinking of God as your dad and Jesus as your brother help you feel closer to him?

13

A Safe Place

Trust in him at all times, O people;
   pour out your heart before him;
   God is a refuge for us.

PSALM 62:8

Erin is sitting on her bed. She hates bedtime more than anything. She feels the familiar scary thoughts creeping into her head. It seems that every night she has to fight against thinking about spiders or snakes. The dark has always made her scared. She tries to remember what her parents have said to her about God's taking care of her. God does not feel close right now though; the only thing that feels close are her thoughts. Erin tries to pray, but she can't even think of what to say to God; all she wants is to be next to her parents. She feels so safe with them.

Our verse, Psalm 62:8, talks about God's being a refuge. The way God is described in this verse is perfect for Erin. A refuge is kind of like a fort; it is a safe place. A refuge is a special place where you can go to be protected. The words in our verse are for Erin and for you if you get scared too. We can trust in God; we can tell him that we are scared, and then we can hide in our safe place. Our safe place is God. There is no one who loves you more than he does, and there is no one stronger than him. He will help you through whatever scary or sad things might come into your life. He loves to hear you talk to him about everything. He loves to hear what you are scared of. Think of all your scary thoughts as though they were orange juice in a pitcher, and then think of pouring all that orange juice into the sink. That is what he wants you to do with every scary thought you have. Tell it to him. You can be sure that he hears you and that he will love you.

This verse doesn't mean that nothing sad or scary will ever happen to you, but it does mean that in the middle of sad or scary things you have a place you can go. You have someone to talk to. You have a powerful, loving God who loves to be your strong fort and your protection.

EXPLORATION TIME

1) Does knowing that God wants to hear all about your fears make you want to talk to him?

2) When you are scared, what are the thoughts that bother you most?

3) What is the best and strongest refuge you can think of? Try to think of God this way whenever you are scared.

14

It's Not My Fault!

We know that a person is not justified by works
of the law but through faith in Jesus Christ, so
we also have believed in Christ Jesus.

GALATIANS 2:16

"It isn't my fault!" Joel screams. "He started it when he
took my ball!"

"But you weren't playing with it!" James yells back.

The arguing goes on, back and forth, until their mom
finally says, "No more! I can't handle this anymore! Stop
yelling at each other and go to your rooms!"

Both boys stomp off to their rooms. Anger is bubbling
over in each boy. They both think they have a right to the
ball and can't understand why their mom doesn't see that.
Joel just wants to sit and explain to his mom why it is okay
for him to grab his own ball. James can't understand why
his mom is mad at him; after all, it was Joel who came in
and pushed him.

Believe it or not, Galatians 2:16 can help the boys with
the argument. Both boys are trying to justify themselves.

Here we find another one of our big words: "justified." *Justify* means making sure you are right. So how does our passage help? We have to believe that we aren't right but that Jesus came to make us right. Jesus makes us right before God by living the way we are supposed to live.

Jesus makes us right by dying the death we deserved to die. When we sin, when we are selfish, or when we are angry, we can admit that we have done something wrong. Our passage tells us that we can admit it, because the only one who really matters says we are okay with him now. We are justified by having faith in Christ. We don't have to pretend we don't sin or cover up our sin. Jesus came to cover up our sinfulness for us.

You can never do all the right things. Our treasure map tells us that we don't find happiness in thinking we are always right. We find happiness in knowing that Jesus was always right for us, and he gives us his righteousness. Joel and James and even their mom can admit their sin, their wrongs, to each other and go to Jesus together. God is the one who knows all the wrong in our hearts and loves us anyway.

EXPLORATION TIME

1) What does the word *justify* mean?

2) Do you have a hard time admitting you are wrong?

3) How does knowing that Jesus justifies you help you to admit when you sin?

15

The Lie

Do not lie to one another, seeing that you have put off the old self with its practices and have put on the new self, which is being renewed in knowledge after the image of its creator.

COLOSSIANS 3:9–10

Darrin knows he has been caught. He has the money in his pocket, and his dad is asking him to give it back. He has told his dad over and over again that he didn't take the five dollars that had been on the table, but somehow his dad knows he has been lying. His heart feels as though it weighs one hundred tons. He knows his dad is going to be so disappointed in him. He just really wants that new Lego mini-figure, and the five dollars would buy it for him. All of his friends have been asking him when he is going to get it. He wants to be able to play with them, and he can't without the mini-figure. He has lied because he doesn't want to get in trouble but also because he wants to play with his friends.

Darrin thinks his treasure is having people think good thoughts about him. He wants his friends to think he is cool, which is why he stole the money. He wants his dad to think he is a good boy, which is why he lied about the money. He needs to hear about his Creator. God's opinion is the only one that matters, and God's opinion about Darrin is that Darrin is a new self. Once Darrin trusted Jesus as his Savior, God looked at Darrin as he looks at his Son. Darrin also needs to remember that God takes care of his family and gives them everything they need. So Darrin doesn't have to steal in order to get something he thinks he needs. He can trust God to give him all. Darrin doesn't have to lie to his dad.

When we trust that God loves us no matter what, we can be honest about what we do wrong. We don't have to cover up our sins anymore, because Jesus covered them for us on the cross. That is what it means to be a new self. All of our old, bad sins are forgiven; we are totally new. If Darrin isn't a Christian, then he will spend the rest of his life trying to cover up the sins he does. His lying will not be enough to fool anyone on the day that God will judge him. He has to have a new self, and that is given to anyone who believes. The truth about God's love can help Darrin tell the truth.

EXPLORATION TIME

1) Can you think of a time when you lied because you didn't want to get in trouble?

2) How does knowing God's love for you help you when you want to lie?

3) When you lie, what will help you to come back and tell the truth?

4) If you are a Christian, does God love you any less when you lie?

16

The Blow-Up

> When he was reviled, he did not revile in return; when he suffered, he did not threaten, but continued entrusting himself to him who judges justly.
>
> I PETER 2:23

Paul feels that he can't control himself any longer. Kent has been making fun of him all day. All their classmates keep laughing at Paul. Paul has been trying to be a good sport about it. He has tried to laugh with everyone else, but he is now done with that. He has asked Kent several times to stop, and Kent just responded in a very whiny voice, "Kent, please stop." Paul's fists are balling up, and he decides if Kent calls him a bad word one more time, he will punch him right in the face. Paul knows it isn't right to hit Kent, but at this point he really doesn't care.

Paul needs Jesus. In our verse, 1 Peter 2:23, we hear about how Jesus handled people who made fun of him. What you and I need to understand is that Jesus's suffering was way worse than any unkind way a friend has treated us at school. The people who made fun of Jesus did it at his death. They did it at the worst point of his life. They did it because they hated Jesus and they wanted him to hurt all over. They wanted to hurt his body, and they wanted to hurt his heart. They said the most awful things to Jesus while they were punching him and whipping him.

Our verse tells us how Jesus treated them. It says that when "he was reviled, he did not revile in return." Here is another fancy word, "revile." That word means that they said and did all sorts of awful things to Jesus. But Jesus did not say or do hurtful things in return. We learn that when Jesus was suffering and hurting because of those people, he did not threaten them. I know that when I am being hurt, I want to hurt people back. Jesus had all the power in the world, and he chose not to use it to hurt people. He chose to use that power to help people. How did Jesus do that? He trusted that God would take care of him. So how can we be kind when people hurt us? We can trust that God's love for us is better than anything in this world. We can trust that his love and care for us will be enough. In the end, God will make all the wrongs right; he will make all the sad things come untrue.

There is one more really neat thing about this verse. If you are a Christian, this verse is how God sees you, too. He sees you as hidden in Christ's perfect life. He sees you as never having threatened or hurt anybody with your words. How cool is that? It makes me want to love my friends, because I know that God will take care of everything for me.

EXPLORATION TIME

1) When people make fun of you, do you want to hurt them back?

2) How does 1 Peter 2:23 help you when you are being hurt by others' words?

3) Do you think you can trust God to take care of you when others are hurting you?

17

Betrayed

For you have died, and your life is hidden with
Christ in God.

COLOSSIANS 3:3

Sally is standing in the girls' bathroom crying. Her tears
make it difficult to see her reflection in the mirror. That is
okay with her though. She can't look at herself because she
is so embarrassed. Sally has just found out that her best
friend, Jane, has been telling all her secrets to a group of
girls in their class. Sally had trusted Jane. She had trusted
her with all the things she didn't want anybody else to
know, but Jane had just betrayed her trust. Sally can't believe it. How could Jane do this to her? How could she be
so mean? Sally believed that they were best friends, and
now she is so angry at Jane. Sally is sure she will never talk
to Jane again. Sally isn't sure how she can even go back into
class. The sound of the bell ringing wakes her up to the fact
that she has to face all those girls right now. She has to go
and sit in her chair, but she isn't sure how she can find the
strength to do it.

Sally has been betrayed, and she needs someone who understands what it is like to have a friend turn against you. Sally needs Jesus. Over and over again we see how Jesus understands everything we go through. Jesus knew the pain of a close friend hurting him. Judas turned Jesus over to the very people who wanted to kill him. Sally wants revenge on Jane; she wants to hurt Jane. Jesus never sinned against Judas.

Sally also has to remember that her life is hidden with Christ in God. That means the only thing that really matters about her doesn't change when her secrets are shared. Her life—all that she truly is—is hidden in Christ. When God looks at her, all he sees is Jesus loving Judas, his betrayer. Sally doesn't have to worry about what her friends think. She can remember that she has a perfect hiding place; she can run to her Savior. As she remembers Jesus's love for her, she can love her friends in return. She can love them without needing them to love her back, because her heart will be so full of God's love for her.

EXPLORATION TIME

1) Have you ever been betrayed by a friend?

2) What do you think Jesus felt when Judas betrayed him?

3) How does knowing that your life is hidden with Christ in God help you when someone betrays you?

18

It's Gone!

Do not lay up for yourselves treasures on earth
. . . but lay up for yourselves treasures in heaven,
where neither moth nor rust destroys and where
thieves do not break in and steal. For where
your treasure is, there your heart will be also.

MATTHEW 6:19–21

Morgan runs through the house crying, "Dad! I can't find
my iPod! I have looked everywhere." Her dad tries to calm
Morgan. He asks all the questions that a parent asks when
a child has lost something, and Morgan answers all the
questions and ends up with her iPod still being lost. They
search high, and they search low. No matter where they
look, it isn't to be found. Morgan can't stop crying. She had
saved all of her money to buy the iPod, and now it is gone.
Morgan is very sad.

Morgan has made her treasure her iPod. Maybe you
don't have an iPod, but I bet you can think right now
of your favorite toy—the one that you think about even
when you aren't playing with it. The problem is, now her

treasure is gone. Morgan needs to hear about her real treasure. There is a treasure that no one can take away. There is a treasure that will never break. That treasure is God. Our ultimate treasure is his love for us. Our ultimate treasure is our relationship with him. I know that can seem far away, but it isn't. It really is the only thing that is going to last in your life forever.

The amazing thing about God is that even when you don't think of him as your treasure, he still thinks of you as his. Even when you think your toys or your special things are more important than God, he still loves you. Isn't his love amazing? I know that when people don't love me back the way I love them, I get angry, but God doesn't. He keeps on loving and treating you like his very special daughter or son. He is our forever treasure.

EXPLORATION TIME

1) What toy or special something would make you very sad to lose?

2) Do you sometimes think that something is more important than God?

3) Does knowing that God loves you, even when you love other things, make you love him more?

4) How can God love you even if you aren't loving him?

19

Controlled

For the love of Christ controls us, because we
have concluded this: that one has died for all,
therefore all have died.

2 CORINTHIANS 5:14

Josh stands screaming, his hands covering his ears. All he
can hear is the sound of his own voice. His eyes are closed,
but he can feel his mom close by, trying to pry his hands
from his ears. Josh is so angry at his mom because she has
told him to do his homework before he can play video
games. This seems really unfair. It is Friday night, and he
has all weekend to do his homework. Josh doesn't want to
talk to his mom, and he doesn't want her to talk to him, so
he has decided that the best way to handle the situation is
to scream. So here he stands, screaming as loud as he can.
Sometimes when he does this, his mom gives him what he
wants, and right now he really wants to play video games.
He doesn't care if he is being disobedient; he doesn't care if
he is being mean to his mom. All he cares about is getting
what he wants.

Now, I am sure you can see how Josh is being very naughty. But can you also see how our verse, 2 Corinthians 5:14, would help Josh? Josh needs to hear about a love greater than the one he has for his video games. Our verse tells us about the greatest love that ever existed. It tells us about a love that died for us, a love that gave everything for us. Because of this love we can live, we are forgiven, and we are changed.

The beginning of our verse is very interesting. It talks about how this love, Christ's love for each of his children, controls us. Sometimes when we want something really, really badly, we let it control us. We let what we want change the way we act, and we decide we are willing to do anything to get it. We must remember that our treasure always controls us. In the middle of thinking that getting what we want is our treasure, we must remember that the only true treasure is Christ's love. Remembering what he has done for us and how he gave up things he wanted for our sake will change our hearts. We can't just stop loving video games or whatever else it is in our heart that we love. We must love something more than we love ourselves. That is what changes our hearts. His love can control us, because it is the biggest, strongest love of all. The more we think about his big, strong love for us, the more everything else in this world will lose its control over us.

The really amazing thing is that even as we choose other things to control us and other things to love, he still loves us. Jesus Christ spent his whole life choosing to love instead of choosing his own way, so that we could have his perfect record. That record is yours if you believe his love is for you and that you don't deserve that love but that he has given it to you anyway.

EXPLORATION TIME

1) Are there things in your life besides Christ's love that control you? What are they? What is the most important thing to you right now?

2) How does thinking about Christ's love and his life make you love him more?

20

Not Like Them

Now it is evident that no one is justified before God by the law, for "The righteous shall live by faith."

GALATIANS 3:11

Daniel can't believe those boys are talking like that again. They always use bad language. They always talk about things that are inappropriate. He hates being around them. He just can't understand why they think using those words is okay. Daniel never uses bad words. He also never does anything that his parents might disapprove of. He always feels a little out of place, but he knows it is okay as long as he is doing the right thing. He knows he is better than these boys, and he decides not to talk to them anymore.

Even though it looks like Daniel is a good boy, his heart is far from loving God. Daniel wants to feel good about himself. Daniel always feels good when he does the right thing. The problem is, Daniel is trying to make God love him more by not being like the naughty kids. Daniel doesn't believe Galatians 3:11. He doesn't know or believe that he can't make God love him more by being a rule keeper. That is what the beginning of our verse says: "No one is justified before God by the law." That just means that you won't be accepted by God by keeping all the rules.

The real problem is that even when you think you are keeping all the rules, you aren't. There are so many rules and more rules that there is only one person who could keep them all. That one person was Jesus. He came to keep all the rules in our place, because we can't. Even though it looks like Daniel is keeping all the rules, he has forgotten about loving God and forgotten about loving others.

The next part of our verse tells us how we can be right with God, how we can know without any second-guessing that God loves us. Are you ready for it? All you have to do is have faith. You just believe that God loves you as much as he says he does. You must believe that he sent Jesus to keep all the rules and then to take the punishment for our failing to keep the rules. If you believe that, you are righteous before God. He can never love you more and never love you less. He loves you completely right now. That is really cool, isn't it? The truth of God's love for you should move your heart to want to obey the rules. But you can remember even when you mess up or disobey that God still loves you completely right now.

EXPLORATION TIME

1) Do you think that when you are good, God loves you more?

2) When you are around people who are not acting in a good way, how do you feel?

3) Have you ever prayed for your friends who are being naughty?

4) How does the truth that God loves you completely right now help you when you want to disobey or obey?

21

Forgiveness

[Bear] with one another and, if one has a complaint against another, [forgive] each other; as the Lord has forgiven you, so you also must forgive.

COLOSSIANS 3:13

Quincy is so angry at Carson. Carson has copied him again. Now, this may not seem like a big deal, but Quincy has asked Carson over and over and over again not to copy him. Quincy just doesn't understand why Carson keeps doing it. What makes it even worse is that Carson feels bad about what he has done and has asked Quincy to forgive him. But Quincy doesn't want to forgive Carson. Quincy wants to be mad at Carson. He feels that he has forgiven him so many times for this very thing that he should not have to forgive him anymore.

Quincy needs to be reminded of how Christ has forgiven him. He needs to hear about the great unending supply of forgiveness that God has ready to give to him. Our verse, Colossians 3:13, tells us that we need to bear with one another, which just means to love someone even when it is really hard. Our verse also tells us that we must forgive each other. Now, that is really, really, really hard to do when someone keeps sinning against us.

The really cool thing is that our verse doesn't just say, "FORGIVE AND LOVE!" It also reminds us of the good news: "The Lord has forgiven you." Wow! For all the times you are angry and don't want to forgive, the Lord has forgiven you. For all the times you are the one being annoying and unkind, the Lord has forgiven you. For all the times you have disobeyed your parents or lied or hurt someone or stolen something, "the Lord has forgiven you." When you feel like you can't forgive someone, or you don't want to forgive someone, you can remember those words. You can remember that the Lord has forgiven you.

If you stacked up all of your sins against God, it would go to the moon and back about a billion times. If you stacked up every time that your brother or sister or friends or parents sinned against you, it would probably just go to the top of a mountain. God has forgiven you more than you could ever forgive someone else. He just loves you that much, and he is just that good. When you see all that you have been forgiven, you will find it much easier to forgive others. Remembering his forgiveness and love over and over and over again will help you to be able to love and forgive too.

EXPLORATION TIME

1) Do you ever feel that you don't want to forgive someone? Why?

2) How does thinking about God's forgiveness help you when someone has been unkind to you?

3) What are the words you need to remember when someone asks for your forgiveness?

22

The Bad Report Card

And the life I now live in the flesh I live by
faith in the Son of God, who loved me and gave
himself for me.

GALATIANS 2:20

Chris sits in his room alone. He has never felt so alone.
He has disappointed his parents by bringing home a bad
report card. It is the worst report card he has ever had.
He knows it is his fault, and he knows that everyone is
really upset with him. Chris isn't sure that his parents still
love him; even if they do, their love seems really far away.
It seems that nobody really loves him or cares about how
he feels or what he is going through. Chris even feels that
maybe God doesn't really love him anymore. How could
God love someone who has screwed up as much as he has?
Chris tries to tell himself that being loved doesn't matter.
He will grow up someday and move out of the house and
not have to worry about grades. He will find friends who

care about him, no matter what. He will find a girl who will always be there for him. He won't need his parents, or God—he will make it on his own.

Chris is playing funny tricks in his mind. First, he is telling himself that nobody loves him and that he doesn't need love. Then he is telling himself he will find love when he gets older. Chris really does want to be loved, and he really is loved. He has just forgotten about the most important love ever.

Sometimes when I am feeling very lonely and angry, I, too, forget about the most important love ever. Listen to what we read in Galatians 2:20. Christ loved me and gave himself for me. Chris thinks no one cares, no one loves, and no one will do anything for him. The truth is that Chris has already been cared for and loved, and someone gave his very life for Chris. I know that sometimes God's love feels really far off; it's almost like saying the stars love us. It's like it really doesn't matter. But I promise— it matters more than anything else. It matters because now you can have a forever love. It matters because God sees everything about you, all the nasty, mucky mud in your heart, and he still chooses to love you. It matters because his love cleans the nasty muck and gives you a new, shiny heart.

When you are feeling unloved, when you are feeling that there is not a person in the whole entire world who cares about you, you can remember the end of our verse: Christ loves you. That thought will be able to help you live your life for him. With his help, it will move your heart away from yourself and enable you to believe that his love is true.

EXPLORATION TIME

1) Does God's love for you seem far away or close?

2) When his love seems far away, what can you do to remember the truth?

3) How does thinking about his love and all he gave of himself for you help you when you are lonely?

23

The Saddest Day

He will wipe away every tear from their eyes,
and death shall be no more, neither shall there
be mourning, nor crying, nor pain anymore, for
the former things have passed away.

REVELATION 21:4

Clara is devastated. She has never been so sad in all of her
life. She just found out that her grandma has died. Her
parents said that Grandma "has gone to her real home"
and that she is "with Jesus." Clara knows that those words
should make her feel better, but they just don't. She wants
to be with her grandma. She wants to hold her hand and
hear her laugh. The hurt that is inside her heart just won't
stop. She feels that she doesn't have enough tears to cry.
Clara knows her life will never be the same. She misses
her grandma so much. Every time she sees her mom cry, it
makes it harder. She knows her mom is trying to hide her
tears and to keep life going on as normal. The problem is, it
isn't normal, and Clara thinks it will never be normal again.
One of the things she has loved most about her grandma is

how Grandma always loved on her when she was sad. Clara just doesn't know who will love her now.

It is right for Clara to be sad. Clara's grandma was a very special person, and it is okay for Clara to miss her. Our verse, Revelation 21:4, can help the hurt in Clara's heart because it talks about our real home. Heaven seems strange sometimes. It's just so far away and doesn't even seem to make a lot of sense.

There is so much about heaven that we don't know and won't understand until we are there, but one thing we do know is found in our verse: there is no crying in heaven. The Bible says that God himself will wipe every tear from our eyes. How gentle and tender is that thought? God cares about our tears. He is the best treasure of all! In heaven there will be no more death. We will be with the ones we love the most forever. In heaven, all the things we have loved more than God will be seen for the silly things they really are.

In heaven, there will also be no more pain. Clara will never feel the pain that is in her heart ever again. Clara's grandma will never feel the pain of getting old and having her body not work the way it should. All the sadness that we know here on earth will be gone. We can look forward to that day. We can hope for that day. And we can know that our God is sweet and loving and beautiful, and he cares about all our sadness. He cares about all our hurt. He is also looking forward to the day when he can wipe our tears away. Clara can have hope in her saddest times, because a day will come when all sadness will die.

EXPLORATION TIME

1) Do you ever think of God as someone who will wipe our tears away?

2) How does Revelation 21:4 help when you are sad?

3) Do you miss someone who has died?

24

The Award

> And Jesus said to him, "Why do you call me good? No one is good except God alone."
>
> MARK 10:18

Maria stands in front of the assembly. She can't help but smile; she can see her parents smiling at her from the audience. She has won the "Christian Character of the Year" award for the fourth-grade girls. Maria knows that winning this award means a big celebration dinner at her favorite restaurant. It means she will get to call her grandparents and tell them the news. She can't wait to get home and put her trophy up in her bedroom. She has tried really hard all year to win this award. She has been nice when people have been mean to her, and she has tried to make good decisions all year long. Now it has paid off. She waves to her mom and hugs her teacher. This is definitely one of the best days of her life.

Sometimes we forget that even on our best days, we still need Jesus. Actually, the truth is that we probably need Jesus more on the days when we think we are good. That's because on the days we think we are good, we don't think much about needing a savior. In our verse, Mark 10:18,

Jesus tells a man in the Bible, who was probably a lot like Maria, that "no one is good except God alone." Maria really needs to hear this, and so do we.

It is dangerous to believe that our goodness makes God love us more. You see, God's love is not like that. God does not love us more on the days when we win awards for being nice, and he doesn't love us less on the days when we mess things up. God just loves us because he decided to love us. God loves us because he is good, not because we are good. Maria can be happy that God helped her to make good decisions all year, but she must not make her goodness the most important thing. When we make our goodness the most important thing, we start to believe that we don't need to be saved from our sins. We might even start to think that we are better than other people, and that is a lie.

The truth is, we all need Jesus. We could never live a perfect life. He had to come and do it for us. The good news is that Jesus won the best award for us—he has given us the award for his perfect life. Our reward is forever with God and forever in his family as one of his loved children.

EXPLORATION TIME

1) Do you ever think that God loves you more when you are good?

2) Why is it right to believe that no one is good but God?

3) Why is it wrong to believe that we can be good enough?

4) How has Jesus been good enough for you?

25

Never Enough

Keep your life free from love of money, and be
content with what you have, for he has said, "I
will never leave you nor forsake you."

HEBREWS 13:5

Robert really wanted a new Lego set. It doesn't cost very
much money, and he did a bunch of little jobs around the
house so that he could buy it. The day finally came when
he had enough money, and his mom took him to the store
to buy it. Robert was so excited to come home and build
it, and it didn't take very long to put it all together. He has
been sitting in his room for hours playing with it. He really
loves it, and he is really happy.

Later that day, his dad brings the mail into the kitchen
and lays it on the counter. There in the mail Robert sees one
of his favorite things to look at—the new Lego magazine.
There on the cover is a set he has never seen before. He
can't believe how cool it looks. The mini-figures are brand-
new too. Robert gets a sinking feeling in his stomach. Why
did he spend all his money on that old set? If he had just

waited, he could have gotten this new set, and he would have been the only boy on his street to have it. He decides to start saving money again so he can buy the new Legos.

Robert has absolutely, positively made Legos his treasure. He keeps thinking that if he just gets the newest set, he will be happy. The problem is that every time he gets the newest set, another newer one comes out. Our verse, Hebrews 13:5, tells us that we should try to keep our lives free from the love of money. We could very easily put Legos or American Girl dolls or a new bike or whatever in that verse instead of the words "love of money."

Our verse also tells us to be content with what we have. Now, I am here to tell you that I am not content with what I have all the time. It is so hard to look at what I have and then look at all the cool new things out there and be content. I know I should just be happy with what I have, but when I see a new gadget, I want it. Robert, you, and I need the last part of our verse to help us. The last part of our verse reminds us of what really matters, which is that we already have everything we need. We have a God who promises never to leave us or forsake us. Even when we love things more than we love God, he promises never to leave us or forsake us. Even when we think that only a new Lego set will make us happy, he will never leave us or forsake us. Even when we get angry because we can't have the toy we want, he will never leave us or forsake us. You see, things, toys, gadgets, and gizmos will never really make us happy. Sure, for a little while they are great and fun, but they get old and they break, and something newer and cooler always comes out.

Our hearts were never meant to be satisfied with things that money can buy. Our hearts will only ever be really eternally happy when we remember that our God loves us and will never leave us.

EXPLORATION TIME

1) Do you think that a new toy will make you happy? What is that toy?

2) Does thinking about God's never leaving you or forsaking you make you happy? If it doesn't, why not pray and ask God to show you how awesome that is?

3) Have you ever received a new toy that you thought was amazing and then decided it wasn't that great later?

4) What is the only thing that will really make your heart forever happy?

26

Worried

Trust in the LORD with all your heart,
  and do not lean on your own
    understanding.
In all your ways acknowledge him,
  and he will make straight your paths.

PROVERBS 3:5–6

Sarah walks around gloomy all the time. She always feels that something bad is going to happen. She really can't understand why she feels that way. If her family is about to go on a trip, she worries that they will get in a car accident. On her way to school, she always thinks that her friends are going to be mean to her. After school she worries that she won't be able to get her homework done. On the weekends she is sad because she knows she has to go back to school on Monday. She just always thinks that things are bad, even when they really aren't. Her parents have told her to trust in God. She tries to do that, but she doesn't really know what that means. She doesn't understand how trusting in God will make any difference in her day. So she has given up, and she figures that she is the only little girl who can't understand what that means. She always feels a little sad and a little scared.

Sarah's parents are right. Sarah needs to learn to trust in God. But what does that really mean? How do you trust in God? Our verse, Proverbs 3:5–6, answers those questions. We believe with all of our hearts that God is good and loves us. That is what *trusting* means. We believe that he will always take care of us, even if we get in a car accident, or our friends are mean, or Monday comes and we have to go back to school.

Our verse also tells us something very important about having our hearts full of trust in God: we can't lean on our own understanding. Does that sound silly? Let me explain what that means. It means that we can't think we know how everything will work out. Sarah always thinks the worst things will happen, and then she thinks that no one will know how to help in those bad situations. The Bible tells us that if we believe God is good and that he loves us, he will make our paths straight. That basically means that he will always take care of us, no matter what happens. Even if bad things do happen, he is there with us. We don't have to figure everything out; he already has all of our lives figured out for us. He's got everything under his control, and remember—he is good, and he loves you. He always takes care of his children. He is the best Father ever. You can trust in him to do exactly the best thing.

EXPLORATION TIME

1) Do you understand what it means to trust in God?
Explain it.

2) How does knowing that God knows better than you help
you to trust him?

3) Pray that God will help you to trust him.

27

Bullies

Do not be overcome by evil, but overcome evil
with good.

ROMANS 12:21

Frank watches as his friends make fun of the new boy in
class. It is the first day of school, and it is Jimmy's first day
in this school. Jimmy doesn't look like the other boys; he
is different in every possible way. He is smaller than the
other boys, and he has a different skin color. He dresses differently from the others, and he even talks differently. He
has moved from a different part of the United States, so he
has a "funny" accent. Frank feels bad that his buddies are
being so mean. They call out horrible names and copy the
way Jimmy says certain words. Frank also feels scared; he
doesn't want his buddies to turn on him and decide to make
fun of him too. Frank knows he should tell them to stop,
but he also really likes having friends. So Frank stands qui-
etly. Inside he feels yucky; outside he forces a smile so that
the guys won't know what he is thinking.

Frank knows the right thing to do. He needs to stand

up for Jimmy, but he can't find the courage to do it. Frank needs help to be courageous. He needs the Holy Spirit to come into his heart and remind him of the bravest thing that ever happened in all of history. Frank needs to remember the bravest man in all of history. Jesus was the one who stood up to evil and defeated evil.

Our verse, Romans 12:21, uses the word *overcome*. Do you know what that word means? It means to "defeat" or "overwhelm." In really understandable words, it means to "beat." That is what Jesus did to evil—he beat it. He beat it in the strangest way; he beat it by doing good. Most of the time we think we can beat evil by being meaner or being stronger, but Jesus beat evil by goodness and by dying. He beat Satan by giving his life on the cross and by giving us the forgiveness we need for all the times we are evil.

If Frank would remember this, he would be able to stand up to his friends, no matter what. Frank could tell his friends that what they are doing is wrong, and he could go to Jimmy and try to be his friend. He could overcome evil with good. Doing the right thing can be really hard, especially when we have to go against what our friends are doing, but doing the right thing reminds us of what Jesus did for us. Jesus stood up for us. He took all our punishment. He loved us when we were the bad guys. And he did all of that to make us his friends. Sometimes the right thing is the hardest thing, but in those times we can know that Jesus understands how difficult it is and that he is praying for us right at that moment.

EXPLORATION TIME

1) Have you or your friends ever made fun of people because they are different from you?

2) What would give you the courage to stand up for someone who was being made fun of?

3) How did Jesus stand up for you?

28

Finishing the Level

He who did not spare his own son but gave him
up for us all, how will he not also with him graciously give us all things?

ROMANS 8:32

Noah cannot believe how mean his parents are being. He
just wants 10 minutes of extra video-game time. They always have all these ridiculous rules that he doesn't understand. Noah feels that he never gets what he wants. He feels
that his parents love to make him mad. So Noah does what
he knows will work—he starts asking over and over and
over again for 10 more minutes. He decides he won't stop
until they say yes. The problem is, they keep saying no.
Noah really feels that if gets that extra 10 minutes, he will
finish the level he is on. He really just doesn't understand
why he can't have what he wants.

Noah has made what he wants into his treasure. He really has no room in his heart for anything other than playing video games. He feels that if he could just have what
he wants, he would be a better boy. Noah has decided that
what God has given to him isn't enough.

I sometimes feel like Noah. I forget the truth of Romans 8:32. I forget that God has given me everything I need, and I look for other things to make me happy. Noah feels that nobody cares about what he wants. The truth is, God does care about what we want. He knows that what we want is to be happy. He also knows the thing that will make us the happiest is himself. We think that finishing a video-game level or getting a certain dress or having friends come over will make us happy, but God tells us in this verse that he has given us everything we need to be happy. He didn't spare his own Son. He sent the one he loved most to live every day perfectly content and to die for our discontentment. He did that so that we could know true happiness.

True happiness is knowing that the God who created the universe cares specifically about us and will take care of all our needs. You can know right now, this very second, that everything you need, you already have. All your needs are completely taken care of. You can remember this when you feel that there is something you really need but aren't getting. You can remember that God graciously gave you his Son; he will also give you everything else you need.

EXPLORATION TIME

1) What are some things that you want but don't have right now?

2) How will knowing that God gave his Son help you when you want something you can't have?

3) Does thinking about God's generosity help you to believe that he will take care of you?

29

Just Not Fair

Praise the LORD!
Oh give thanks to the LORD, for he is good,
    for his steadfast love endures forever!

PSALM 106:1

"I hate broccoli!"

"Why do I have to take a shower now?"

"When can I watch my show? We always watch your show!"

Julie is having a hard night. She feels that whenever she wants something, her parents always say no. She has told her mom over and over again that she hates broccoli, and her mom still served it. She was right in the middle of playing a game when her dad told her to take a shower. The worst part of her night was that after her shower, she just wanted to watch her favorite show, but her parents were watching something else. That just sent Julie over the edge. She is so angry. She can't think of anything to be happy about. Her mom keeps telling her that she has so much to be grateful for, but Julie can't think of one thing. All she can think of are the things that haven't gone the way she wanted. Julie feels that her parents enjoy making her life miserable.

Our verse, Psalm 106:1, is what Julie's heart needs to hear. She has forgotten the most important thing in the entire world, which is that the Lord is good, and his love for her will never, ever stop. God's love will keep chasing her even when she hates the food her parents make. God's love will still continue even when she wants to disobey her parents. God's love will love Julie forever.

Does that seem a bit extreme? Don't you think that God would get mad at Julie because she forgets about his love? God's love is not like our love. God's love will endure forever, because that is how much he loves Jesus. Jesus was always grateful and never complained. Jesus was a little boy, and I am sure that there were foods his mom made that he didn't like, but instead of screaming at his mom, he ate with gratitude. That seems impossible to me. There are some foods that seem just too icky to eat.

Jesus did this so that God's love for you would always be there. There was a time when Jesus asked God to take a cup away from him. Jesus was praying right before he was crucified, and Jesus was scared of what was about to happen to him. He knew that God was going to punish him for all of our sins, for our ingratitude. Jesus gave his life for us so that in our moments of complaining and ingratitude we can know that God still loves us. He took our punishment, and he lived a life of complete gratitude.

Friends, when we look at Jesus's life and see all that he did and hear about God's love, our hearts should be grateful. So the next time there is broccoli on your plate, think of our verse. Think of our God's great love and plug your nose and eat the broccoli.

EXPLORATION TIME

1) Are there days when you just feel angry about everything? On those days, can you promise to pray with someone?

2) How does remembering how Jesus lived help you to be grateful?

3) How does remembering that God's love goes on forever help you to be grateful?

4) When you aren't grateful, does God's love for you change?

30

The Ten-Dollar Bill

No temptation has overtaken you that is not common to man. God is faithful, and he will not let you be tempted beyond your ability, but with the temptation he will also provide the way of escape, that you may be able to endure it.

1 CORINTHIANS 10:13

Rachel looks at the ten-dollar bill lying on the floor. She knows it is her dad's, but she also knows that he would never even realize that it is gone. It had fallen out of his pocket on his way out the door. Rachel was the only one who saw it happen. She has been saving money for a necklace she really wants, and she is only six dollars short. If she takes the money, then she can go buy the necklace. She feels awful inside; she knows stealing is wrong. But she also feels excited; she really wants that necklace. Her longing for the necklace is bigger than anything else, so she reaches down, picks up the money, and puts it in her pocket.

Rachel has made a treasure out of the necklace. She has decided that it is the most important thing in her life, and she will do anything to get it. She feels that she has no choice; she has to steal the money. She thinks nobody understands how badly she wants that necklace. Rachel ignores all the feelings that tell her that stealing is wrong. Rachel needs our verse, 1 Corinthians 10:13, to be in her head today. She needs to hear that God can help her through the desire to steal.

God promises that he is always faithful to us. Every time we face a choice between right and wrong, he has made a way for us to do the right. If you are a Christian, if you are a son or daughter of God, he has given you help. That help is the Holy Spirit. He is always with you and in you telling you when you should obey God. Rachel ignored what was right. The amazing thing is that God still remains faithful to her. He gives her opportunity to tell her parents what she has done wrong. God's love for her never stops. His care for her, even when she is stealing, goes on forever. And the Holy Spirit will continue to remind her that stealing is wrong.

Do you know that feeling you get when you are disobeying, the one that makes you feel so icky inside? That is God working in your heart to help you want to do the right thing. Any time you are tempted with stealing or lying or whatever, you can know that God is bigger and stronger than everything. He can help you to do the right thing, even if it is really hard. He can help you remember that his love and faithfulness are the most important things of all.

EXPLORATION TIME

1) Do you feel bad when you do something wrong? If not, maybe you aren't a Christian. You can pray right now that God will make you one of his children.

2) How does thinking about God's faithfulness to you help you to make the right decision?

3) Is there a situation in your life right now in which you are trying to decide between doing the right thing and doing the wrong thing?

31

Lots of Icing

For even the Son of Man came not to be served but to serve, and to give his life as a ransom for many.

MARK 10:45

Samantha pushes her way to the front of the line. She wants to make sure that she gets the corner piece of cake. She loves frosting. She accidentally steps on her little brother's foot, and he starts crying—again. Samantha gets so sick of him crying at the littlest things.

"Samantha is pushing, Mom!" His little voice fills up the whole kitchen.

"Great, here comes Mom," Samantha thinks. "Now I won't get that piece of cake!"

Just then she looks up, and Uncle James is handing her the piece she has wanted. She grabs it quickly, too quickly. The piece falls on the ground just as her mom grabs her arm. Samantha can't believe it. She is so angry—angry at her brother, angry at her mom. Why can't everyone just leave her alone?

The delicious corner piece of cake filled up Samantha's heart and mind. She wanted that cake so badly; she didn't care what she had to do to get it. She really didn't think it was that big of a deal to push to the front of the line. She knew no one else liked the corner piece as much as she did. Her little brother was always getting in the way and always making a big deal out of nothing. Samantha's mind and heart were filled with the desire to be first and to get the best for herself, which is why she needs to hear our verse, Mark 10:45. She needs to hear about Jesus, how he came to earth to serve her.

Jesus came to earth to be a servant. He was the only one who has ever deserved the best of everything, because he was the only one truly good. Instead of demanding the best, he came to give. He gave every second of every day up until the day he died. He gave so that he could give his life as a "ransom for many." Those words are hard to understand, so let me tell you what they mean. A ransom is what you pay to get a prisoner free, and you are actually the prisoner. You are a prisoner to sin and death. Jesus came to set you free. He came to set you free from always wanting the best for yourself. He came to set you free from feeling that being first is better. He paid the hugest price to give you freedom from always thinking of yourself.

Thinking about how Jesus was a servant should move your heart to want to be a servant. It should help you to see that getting the biggest piece of cake or the best seat or playing with the best toy isn't the most important thing. Jesus's love for you is the most important thing. Guess what? You have his love, so now you can give up all the less important things without worrying about yourself. His love is enough to make you happy forever.

EXPLORATION TIME

1) Do you have a hard time giving up what you think is the best?

2) How did Jesus live as a servant?

3) What does *ransom* mean? How did Jesus pay the ransom for your life? How can this help you to be a servant to others?

32

Test Day

Fear not, for I am with you;
    be not dismayed, for I am your God;
I will strengthen you, I will help you,
    I will uphold you with my righteous
        right hand.

ISAIAH 41:10

It is test day for Adrian. He has been dreading this day for two weeks now. Adrian has struggled through his science class all year. He has a terrible grade, and today's test will either help him pass or really hurt. If he doesn't pass the test, his summer is going to be awful because he will have to go to summer school. He really doesn't see how he can possibly pass the test, so in his mind he goes through every possible excuse for why he shouldn't have to take the test or even go to school today. His parents will not listen. They keep telling him that he will do fine and that God will help him to remember all that he has studied. Adrian knows his parents don't understand. He knows that when he sits down and looks at that test, everything he has studied will run from his mind. It will all disappear like it always does.

He feels hopeless and angry and sad and just wants to run and hide.

Adrian really needs to hear some good news. The good news he needs to hear is that God will be there to help him. Now, that doesn't mean that he will pass the test; he may end up having to go to summer school. It does mean that even if he doesn't pass the test, God will be with him during the test and during summer school. Adrian feels that the test will be the hardest thing he has ever had to do, and that makes him feel so alone. He is forgetting that Jesus Christ understood exactly what he is going through.

Jesus knew what it was like to do things that seem impossible. He knew what it was like not to want to do something that he had to do. Right before Jesus was crucified, he prayed that if there was any way to avoid going through it, God would let that happen. Then he prayed that he would do what God planned for him to do. Jesus understands Adrian. Jesus understands you, and he understands me. He promises to be with us always, and the Bible tells us he is praying for us in every situation.

Our verse, Isaiah 41:10, doesn't say that we will pass every test because of God's giving us strength or that every hard thing we do will turn out just right. It does promise us that in all our difficulties, we will have God with us. He will give us strength to go through it all. The Holy Spirit is our helper and always there when we need him. So in our hardest times, on the days when we just wish we could disappear instead of going to school, we can absolutely know that God is with us and loves us. He promises us that, and he always keeps his promises.

EXPLORATION TIME

1) Is there anything coming up in your life that you are scared of doing?

2) How does knowing that God gives you strength help when you have to do something hard?

3) How can knowing that Jesus understands how you feel help you on difficult days?

33

Champions!

Indeed, I count everything as loss because of
the surpassing worth of knowing Christ Jesus
my Lord. For his sake I have suffered the loss of
all things and count them as rubbish, in order
that I may gain Christ.

PHILIPPIANS 3:8

Justice runs into the center of the field with all his teammates. They have just won the championship game. Justice
has had the best game of the entire season. He sacked the
quarterback twice, and he even had a touchdown, his first
of the season. All his coaches are slapping him on the back,
telling him he had a great game. He looks over to the side-
lines, and there he sees his dad cheering. Justice waves and
his dad comes running onto the field, bends down, and gives
Justice a huge hug, and Justice is so happy that he doesn't
even care if his friends saw. He really can't believe that they
won. He has worked so hard for this win, and now he has it.
His day just keeps getting better and better. Then the head
coach gives him the game ball. Justice knows this day will
be one that he remembers forever.

Although Justice doesn't think he has ever been happier, he needs to remember that even on the days when he feels like the happiest person alive, he still needs Jesus. The truth is that nothing is worth as much as knowing Jesus. That is what our verse, Philippians 3:8, is about. It tells us that the most important thing in the whole entire world is knowing that Jesus is our Savior. Jesus is just that amazing.

Knowing what God has done to show you his love is better than winning all the football games in all the world. You see, things here on earth are close, and sometimes they make us happy for a little while, but they will never really make us forever happy. God has made you so that you will only be really happy if you have him. So winning is fun and can make you feel good, but that feeling will go away. God's love for you is the only thing that will make you feel good forever. The really good news is you don't have to win to get this love. God just chooses to love you because he is loving and worth all of our love.

EXPLORATION TIME

1) How can you believe that Jesus is worth more than anything?

2) Do you ever feel that the things on this earth make you happier than God does? If you do, why not pray and ask God to show you how amazing he is?

34

Moving Away

Blessed be the God and Father of our Lord Jesus
Christ, the Father of mercies and God of all comfort, who comforts us in all our affliction, so
that we may be able to comfort those who are
in any affliction, with the comfort with which
we ourselves are comforted by God.

2 CORINTHIANS 1:3–4

Jen thinks her heart is actually going to break. Her in-
sides feel horrible. She can't stop crying since she heard
the news. Her best friend, Sarah, is moving away. They
have been neighbors since they were babies. They have
gone to the same church and the same school and spent almost every day together. What will she do now that Sarah
is leaving her? She is mad at Sarah's dad because he has
decided to take a job in a different state. Jen doesn't understand how anybody could think that a job is more important than a friend. Sarah and Jen sit next to each other
holding hands; Sarah is leaving in less than a month. Their
lives and their friendship will be changed forever. Jen just

doesn't know what she will do without Sarah. She isn't sure she will ever find a friend again.

Jen desperately needs comfort. She feels lonely and terribly sad, and she doesn't think anyone can understand how she feels. She is wrong; there is one who completely understands. Our passage, 2 Corinthians 1:3–4, calls him the "Father of mercies." Even though this is a difficult time for Jen, Jesus is with her and understands her sadness.

Have you ever thought about how hard it must have been for Jesus to leave heaven and come to earth? He had always been with God, his Father, and with the Holy Spirit— since forever. He had to leave them to come to earth, so Jesus understands exactly what Jen feels. He also had to leave his friends and family here on earth when he died and went back to heaven. If there was ever anybody who understands the heartache of being away from someone you love, it was Jesus.

The really neat thing is that he promises to comfort us. He promises to be with us in our sadness, in our times of loneliness. He promises to be enough for us. He will be our forever friend who is always with us. He will make our heart feel better with his love. Because of his love, Jen can tell him all about her sadness. She can run to Jesus because he knows what living apart from friends is like, and his care for her will make it better. Jen can learn what it is like to make Jesus her best friend. Then someday when Jen hears about two friends who are going to be separated, she can comfort them the same way Jesus has comforted her. He cares about your sadness; you can go to him.

EXPLORATION TIME

1) Have you ever had to be separated from someone you love? How did you feel?

2) Have you ever thought about how Jesus felt when he had to leave heaven?

3) How does knowing he understands help you?

35

The Batter's Box

But I have trusted in your steadfast love;
my heart shall rejoice in your salvation.

PSALM 13:5

Jeff stands in the batter's box. He can feel his heart pounding in his chest. There are two outs, and his friend Lance is standing on third base. He can hear his dad yelling, "You've got this, Jeff! A base hit will win it!" He can see his coach clapping his hands and giving him the sign to hit the ball. Jeff has two strikes and three balls on him. He takes a couple of practice swings and waits for the pitch. The pitcher looks at him, and Jeff can tell that he is just as nervous. He sees the ball release from the pitcher's hand and come toward the plate. Jeff decides to swing. He swings with all his might and hears a sentence that breaks his heart: "Strike three, you're out!" The game is over. Jeff stands there shocked. It is his fault they have lost. His team will be mad, his coach will be disappointed, and he doesn't even want to think about what his dad will say. Jeff turns to go back to the dugout with his eyes on the ground. He doesn't think he will ever be able to look any of his teammates in the eye today.

Jeff needs to hear that he is loved even though he made the last out. Our verse, Psalm 13:5, would help Jeff get through this painful day. Jeff has God's steadfast love, whether he struck out or made the winning hit. That word "steadfast" is a really neat word that people don't use a lot anymore. It means that the love God has for Jeff and for all his children will never, ever, ever end. It also means that God's love for you doesn't change. So if you are the hero of the game or the worst player on the team, God loves you the same. Always.

Jeff doesn't know how his team will treat him, but he can be certain that God will treat him with the same love as he always does. That is what it means to trust in steadfast love. You too can know that God absolutely, positively will never stop loving you. You can trust that.

The next part of our verse tells us the way this should make you feel. It says, "I will rejoice." The news of God's love should make a smile appear on your face. Now, I know that in the moment of striking out and losing a game, a smile isn't the best thing to wear. But you can smile in your heart, knowing that the most important thing about you isn't how you play baseball or any sport. The most important thing about you is God's love for you. You can smile because that will always be yours.

EXPLORATION TIME

1) Can you think of a time when you were sad because you felt that you disappointed a team?

2) How can remembering God's steadfast love help you?

3) Is God's steadfast love for you enough to make you smile? If not, please pray that it would be enough.

36

Applesauce Disaster

It is better to take refuge in the LORD
  than to trust in man.

PSALM 118:8

Teresa feels the applesauce dripping from her pants into her shoes. She can also feel her cheeks starting to burn with embarrassment. She has done it again. She has hit her applesauce while talking, and it has fallen right into her lap. All her classmates are laughing at her. She hates that she is so clumsy. She doesn't understand why she is the only one who always trips and does stupid things like this. She feels about 2 inches tall; she actually wishes she were that small so she could run away without anybody seeing her. Teresa wants to disappear; instead, she has to stand up in front of everyone and go get napkins to clean off her pants. She knows that all her friends will keep bringing it up and making fun of her. She really wants to hide for the rest of the day—or maybe even for the rest of her life.

Teresa does need a place to hide; she needs our verse, Psalm 118:8. Here we have another fancy word, *refuge*; it means "a shelter from danger." Imagine the biggest, strongest castle you can think of, one that no one could ever break into—a castle surrounded by a big moat with crocodiles in it and strong soldiers standing guard. That is what a refuge is. Our verse tells us to take refuge in the Lord. Imagine him as your castle.

That may seem a little bit silly; how can you take refuge in the Lord when you have applesauce squishing in your shoes? You take refuge by remembering that he is your treasure. You remember that he never laughs at you, that his love for you doesn't change on the days when you do everything perfectly, and it doesn't change on the days when everything is a jumbled-up mess. When you are sure of his love, you don't have to worry about or trust in what other people think of you. Instead, you can be sure that you have the most powerful, best person on your side, even if everyone else is laughing at you.

EXPLORATION TIME

1) Do others laugh at you so that you think you are not loved?

2) How would thinking about God as your castle help you?

3) Does God's love make a difference on the days when you feel left out?

37

Admitting Wrong

If we confess our sins, he is faithful and just to forgive us our sins and to cleanse us from all unrighteousness.

1 JOHN 1:9

Craig is feeling really sad, like, you-can-barely-lift-your-head-up sad. He knows he has been mean to his sister, and he knows that she is crying in the other room. She had been playing with his toys, and he got really angry and yelled some very awful things at her. She ran out crying, and Craig went and hid in the closet. His parents have always told him that if he is unkind to someone, he should ask for forgiveness. He knows that he should go right up to his sister and say, "Please forgive me for being unkind." The problem is, he just doesn't want to. Well, part of him does, but part of him doesn't. Part of him is still mad that she played with his toys; the other part knows that he shouldn't have yelled. He sits in the closet feeling like the darkest of rain clouds.

Craig needs to remember how much he has already been forgiven. He needs to remember the promise that our verse,

1 John 1:9, gives. When we confess or tell God about our sins, he forgives us and makes us totally clean. If Craig could remember this, then he would be able to go and ask his sister to forgive him. You see, when we know how big our sin is and how much God had to do to forgive us for our sins, then little sisters playing with our things don't seem like such a big deal. God's forgiveness is like the biggest ocean on the entire earth, and other people's sin toward us is like a small drop from a faucet.

When we see this, then we are able to be honest about our sin even if others were unkind first. We can go to our brother or sister or mom or dad and just tell it like it is. We can be truthful about how we have messed up, because God has forgiven his kids. He promises that he has forgiven and will keep on forgiving until forever. Asking for forgiveness can be hard, because, if you are at all like me, I don't like to admit I am wrong—ever. But knowing God loves me even when I am wrong and in the times I don't want to admit I am wrong, well, that kind of makes my heart soft. It makes me know it's good to confess and ask for forgiveness. It makes me happy to know that the most important person forgives and loves me always.

EXPLORATION TIME

1) When you sin against someone, what should you do?

2) When you don't feel like asking for forgiveness, what should you do?

3) How does thinking about how you have been forgiven help you to ask for forgiveness from others?

38

The First Shot

Do nothing from selfish ambition or conceit, but in humility count others more significant than yourselves.

PHILIPPIANS 2:3

"ME FIRST!" Jonah screams. He wants to shoot the basketball, but someone else has gotten to it first. Jonah yells again, "Give me the ball! I want it now!" Robby doesn't want to give the ball to Jonah; he had run as fast as he could to get it, and now it is his. Robby hugs the ball close to his chest and makes up his mind that Jonah is not going to get it. The other kids stand around trying to convince Jonah to let Robby shoot it, but Jonah runs over and tries to pull the ball from Robby's hands. Both boys feel anger running through their bodies, and both aren't going to give up. Jonah yanks as hard as he can, but instead of getting the ball loose from Robby, he trips and pulls Robby right on top of him. They both fall to the blacktop. Jonah hits the back of his head and Robby scrapes his knee. Just then Mr. Olson comes out and takes the ball from both boys. He tells them to go inside the classroom, where he will deal with them.

Jonah and Robby had both decided that shooting the basketball first was the most important thing; neither one cared about anything but shooting that basketball. They both need to hear about something that is really important—they both need to hear about Jesus. Our verse, Philippians 2:3, is all about Jesus. It is all about the way Jesus lived every second of every day of his life. He never did anything selfish, and he always made sure that what others wanted was the most important thing.

Stop and think about that for a moment. I don't think I have ever lived even one full day like that. To be really honest, I am not sure I have even lived an hour of my life without doing something selfish. We all think about ourselves the most; it is part of being human. Amazingly, Jesus was human, but he fought the desire to put himself first. He really fought the desire to do what was easy for him when he had to die on the cross. On that day, he had to make the biggest unselfish decision anybody has ever made. He made that decision so that we can be forgiven of all the times we are selfish and want to be first.

The really amazing thing is that if you are one of God's kids, you have Jesus's perfect record of always being unselfish. Even in the times you are selfish, God still loves you. That should make you want to share and think of others instead of yourself. If he has given you that much, you can give to others.

EXPLORATION TIME

1) Think of a time when it was difficult to share. Talk about it.

2) What is the hardest part of putting what others want ahead of what you want?

3) How does thinking about Jesus help you to love others more than you love yourself?

39

The Best Gift

Every good gift and every perfect gift is from above, coming down from the Father of lights with whom there is no variation or shadow due to change.

JAMES 1:17

It is Christmas morning. Darnel has been awake for what seems like hours. His mom had told him that he couldn't come out until 7:00. So he sits staring at the clock. He imagines how incredible it will be if he has gotten the new bike that he has been asking for. He knows that his mom doesn't have a lot of money, but he has hoped and prayed that somehow she could afford it. He can almost feel the wind sweeping across his face as he races his new bike down the street. He blinks and looks over at the clock. The time has finally come. He bursts open the door of his room and runs to the living room—and there it is. His brand-new bike, exactly how he has pictured it, is in the middle of the room. He walks over to it, touching it to make sure it is real, and then turns and runs to his mom. She catches him in a huge embrace, and they laugh. Then she lets him go, and he spends the rest of the day admiring his perfect gift.

Darnel received exactly what he wanted. His mom had saved and worked extra hours to be able to afford it. Our verse, James 1:17, is for Darnel and for all of us this week. It tells us that every good and perfect gift comes down from our Heavenly Father. He loves to give to us and to be generous. Any time you receive a good gift, it should remind you of the best gift that was ever given. Our Heavenly Father gave us the gift of his Son, the gift of forgiveness for sins, the gift of being right with him, and the gift of eternal life.

The next part of our verse is pretty cool, too: there is no change with God. That means that we don't have to wake up in the morning and wonder if God still loves us today. We can know that he doesn't change; he loves us the same today as he did yesterday and the day before and the day before. His feelings for us don't change, because his feelings for Jesus will never change, and we are hidden in Christ. Now, that is a good gift, the best and most perfect gift.

Knowing that we have this forever gift helps us to enjoy all the gifts we get now even more. The gifts we have here will fall apart and break or get lost, but the perfect gift will never, ever be taken from us. So every time we get a good gift, and every time a favorite gift is taken away, we can be grateful that God gave us Jesus, and Jesus will always be ours.

EXPLORATION TIME

1) Is there something you really want right now? What is it?

2) What does James 1:17 tell us about God?

3) Why is it important to know that God doesn't change?

4) What is the best and most perfect gift ever given?

40

The New Baby

See what kind of love the Father has given to us, that we should be called children of God; and so we are.

1 JOHN 3:1

Charlotte watches her mom and dad holding her new little brother. She has been so excited for him to come, but now she is a little sad. She thinks he is cute, and she loves him, but she feels forgotten about. Everyone who has come by the house just wants to see the baby—to hold him and talk about how amazing he is. Charlotte isn't really sure what is so amazing about him; all he does is sleep and cry. She knows she should be happy, but she just feels lonely. She misses her mom and dad holding her and loving her and kissing her. She feels less special and that no one would miss her if she were just to leave. She actually feels that her mom would find it easier if she weren't around asking for things.

Charlotte's world has changed. Her treasure has been her parents' attention and love for her. She has forgotten about her Heavenly Father. She really needs to hear the truth of our verse, 1 John 3:1. She feels unloved, and she must remember how loved she really is.

God loves us so much that he made us his kids. Sometimes we don't see how huge that really is. God didn't have to make us a part of his family. He didn't need us, but he chose to love us, and he decided to tell everyone that he is our dad. Anytime you feel like Charlotte, like you don't belong in a family or that your family doesn't care about you, you can remember this verse. Look at the love God has for you—you are forever his kid. His love is perfect. He is the only perfect Father, and he knows exactly how to love his children just right.

You see, when we remember this, we can love our parents and our brothers and sisters in a different way. We won't love them because of the love they give to us. We will love them because we know that God loves us and that we are his kids. Being part of God's family is eternal. All you have to do to be part of his family is look at his love and believe. You have to know that you don't deserve to be a part of his family, because your sin says you shouldn't go anywhere near God. But because of God's love, he has called you a child. Because Jesus lived the life we should have lived and died the death that we deserved, we can be children of God. Jesus is your brother, and God is your Father. Those two amazing facts can help you if you ever feel a little lost in your family.

EXPLORATION TIME

1) Do you ever feel left out in your family? How does 1 John 3:1 make things better for you in those situations?

2) If God is your Father, do you ever have to worry about not being loved?

Parenting Your Children
with the Love of Jesus

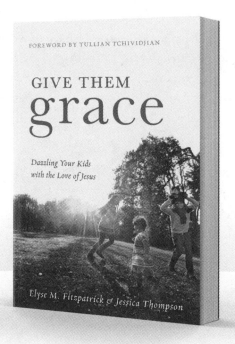

For more information, visit crossway.org.